DISCOVERY IS VITAL

Awaken Love's Inner Voice

Brenda L Balding, RN, MA

DEDICATION

To my dad John A Kaufer [2/22/26-12/12/24 who encouraged me to follow my dreams and mom, Mary Lou Kaufer [1/12/26-3/15/19], who quietly supported us all. [Dad, 7 children, exchange students, travel, 4-year foster sister, a 1500-mile move, and more]. She made it look easy, and I know it was not.

To all who are open to self-reflection and discovery of all parts of YOU, and willing to listen to or awaken "Love's Inner Voice" your cosmic heart.

TABLE OF CONTENTS

Introduction 9

DISCOVER *Enthusiasm* 13

DISCOVER *Should* 19

DISCOVER *Release* 27

DISCOVER *Complacency* 33

DISCOVER *Acceptance* 39

DISCOVER *Forgiveness* 45

DISCOVER *Trust* 51

DISCOVER *Judgment* 57

DISCOVER *Balance* 63

DISCOVER *Connection* 69

DISCOVER *Grief* 75

DISCOVER *Gratitude* 83

Sacred Essence of Words 89

Appendix 93

Acknowledgments 95

About the Author 97

To Err is Human

You may find errors or typos in this book. Please know that they do serve a purpose. The author wanted to write something for everyone, and some "brains" enjoy—even revel—in finding mistakes.

Publisher's Reminder

INTRODUCTION

Welcome to *Discovery is Vital – Awaken Love's Inner Voice*, book two of my "Discovery is..." Series. My mission is to shine light on and share Love's Inner Voice, connection to our Cosmic Heart, for my good, our good, and the highest good of all.

I consider my "Discovery is" series focused journals. *Discovery is Recovery – Brain, Emotion, Spiritual Self-reflection Through the Creative Process*, the first of this series, explores emotions and spiritual concepts. In this book you discover how honesty, hope, faith, courage, integrity, willingness, humility, self-discipline, love, perseverance, spiritual awareness, and service show up in your life.

In *Discovery is Vital – Awaken Love's Inner Voice*, I invite you to notice and possibly heal or surrender what may be blocking you from your sacred story and vital essence. What seeds do you want to nurture within you and share with the world? This is about YOU and how you want to show up in the world.

> VITAL – something is essential or necessary for something to exist or succeed. It can also mean something is full of energy and enthusiasm.
>
> VITAL SYNONYMS – essential, vigorous, needed, key, important, truth
>
> VITAL ANTONYMS – weak, dull, delicate, powerless

The synonyms, antonyms, and some definitions add depth and breadth to the words in this journal for me. My hope is that if the word does not interest you, one of the other words may.

My original title was *Discovery is Vitality*. As I started writing about various words in this focused journal, I realized that they are vital for my transformation.

"Transformation is a process, and as life happens there are tons of ups and downs. It's a journey of discovery – there are moments on mountaintops and moments in deep valleys of despair."

—RICK WARREN

Exploring the ups and downs that showed up has gifted me with increased enthusiasm and continuity of purpose. I find the words essential for my ongoing self-discovery journey of ongoing transformation. Many also assist me to identify what may be decreasing my connection to the "God within," my Love's Inner Voice.

Some daily practices that assist to heal or shine light on my diminished connection to the Divine and *Love's Inner Voice*, are a daily gratitude list, dancing around the house, doodling, EFT[1], walking in nature and taking photos of her beauty, heart breathing, writing, and havening*.

Have fun exploring what is working for you, and what you may want to enhance, let go, or transform as you walk in the light of discovery. Each chapter may be an adventure. Who knows, the vital information about YOU that you discover may be the "key" you need to blossom. This "essential" discovery may be the seed for poems, a memoir, artwork, or… Stay open to all possibilities your brain, emotions, and spirit may reveal.

The primary writing or drawing prompts for your journey are the chapter words, photos, thoughts shared, and whatever questions or feelings you notice. May they open your mind, spirit, and heart to "Love's Inner Voice." Use the blank pages to document your discoveries.

Document with your non-dominant hand to access your subconscious.

It is my hope that *Discovery is Vital – Awaken Love's Inner Voice"* increases your vitality, self-awareness, and expands, energizes, and supports YOU.

---

1   *See Appendix.*

My prayer is that you discover your inner spark or "Love's Inner Voice," then share it with the world. May you experience inner peace, joy, and wonder each day.

Each day of life is an ongoing journey of gratitude, and to identify and transform my blocks from unconditional love and acceptance no matter what. The great gift of a vital life is self-love so I may shine in love and kindness for my good, our good, and the highest good of all.

At the end of each chapter, I have a few questions that may encourage deeper discovery. Add your own questions you wish to explore as they show up on your transformation journey.

Blessings as you journey your unique discovery path to awaken "Love's Inner Voice" within you and connect you to the cosmic heart frequency.

Blessed be, Brenda

Welcome all the visitors that show up "every morning" as Rumi says, in "The Guest House," translated by Coleman Barks.

The Guest House

"This being human is a guesthouse.

"Every morning a new arrival.

"A joy, depression, a meanness, some momentary awareness comes as an unexpected visitor.

"Welcome and entertain them all. Even if they're a crowd of sorrows, who violently sweep your house empty of its furniture, still, treat each guest honorably. He may be clearing you out for some new delight.

"The dark thought, the shame, the malice, meet them at the door laughing, and invite them in.

"Be grateful for whoever comes because each has been sent as a guide from beyond."

—RUMI

Grandpa Love

DISCOVER **ENTHUSIASM**

ENTHUSIASM – The word enthusiasm is derived from the Greek words, en and theos, with theos being the Greek word for God. So "enthusiasm" literally means, in its root concept, "full of God."[2]

My Love's Inner Voice is willing to be "full of God" each day with Godly discernment and cosmic heart connection.

ENTHUSIASM SYNONYMS – fervor, joy, passion, zeal, ardor, spirit

ENTHUSIASM ANTONYMS – apathy, disinterest, hatred, indifference, laziness

*"The word "enthusiasm" comes from the Greek word
"entheos" which means the God within. And the happiest,
most interesting people are those who have found the secret
of maintaining their enthusiasm, that God within."*

—EARL NIGHTINGALE

I n my research about the definition and history of the word "enthusiasm," I found the amazing Earl Nightingale quote. Discovering the joy or passion of being "full of God," identify my true "God within," or my soul. I encourage everyone to identify what "full of God' feels and sounds like to you. I love the sound and feel of the word "entheos" as I say it. I plan to use it throughout this the book.

This photo of my 97-year-old dad with my daughter in June 2023 light up love and enthusiasm for me. Their love for family and each other was electric. Dad loved "dad jokes" and the twinkle in his eyes and the contented posture indicates he just shred one with his granddaughter. He had some smugness when he shared a good joke or insight.

During my ongoing self-discovery journey I realized that I suffered some PTSD related to my marriage. My husband suffered from Vietnam related PTSD that he could not acknowledge and refused to go to counseling with me. My discovery was about emotional and psychological abuse from an unaware and hurting husband, including two STDs. I chose to do many behaviors to keep my marriage together because I was taught marriage was for life. He chose to divorce me to move in with and marry my best friend. When I asked why, he told me, "You don't know how to communicate." My response was, "I guess I do not know how to communicate the way you need me to."

I experienced loss for both my friend, my husband, and my home. He had no interest in sharing custody for our daughter. All he wanted was his small share, due to a second mortgage of the sale of our home.

To get through this and be able to let go of the top layer of pain and shame is the gift of Godly discernment. When the pain or shame is triggered, I have my fullness of God, entheos, when I ask for assistance as I am not God, do not want to be, or am never going to be. This awareness shows me that life's challenges can be a gift to learn from or let go of another layer. God gives me more than I can handle without Godly discernment. What beliefs and behaviors do I have because I have refused challenges given? When I realized this, even a year down the road, fear, apathy or laziness [add your own] may have been driving my bus [me]. I also ask whose thoughts or teaching I am listening to.

What other thoughts or emotions might I be hiding from to keep me from being connected to "entheos"? For me, self-doubt or lack show up when I am in apathy, opposite of entheos. It's important to acknowledge what comes up with a loving "hello, what would you like to let me know?" Listen, and act when indicated. This process also encourages me to notice when I am in creation or what I may want to let go of or transform. Am I in shadow, which is OK, especially when I notice and relax. I did this frequently as a single mom of a 5-year-old. No one in my family was a single parent so I had no one to learn from easily. My beautiful daughter taught me what she needed. I learned love and patience from her and my mom. She also taught me as she got older to let go of needing to fix everything. She would say, in a focused voice, "Mother," when I was overstepping. She has always called me mom or mama, even now. I now ask, "Would you like my thoughts about that?" I do that with others as well. Sometimes I ask, "Would you tell me more about that?" I tend to get over enthusiastic when I think I know the answer to an issue or concern. Usually, the person wishes to figure it out, to learn. When I am in entheos, I listen more deeply from my heart.

We, my daughter and I, had the privilege to live with my parents when we needed to move to San Francisco shortly after my divorce for a daytime job (my daughter was 6). I decided to study statistics as a prerequisite for master's programs, and saving to purchase a condo in the area. I did not know then what I know now about "the God within." I was living one emotional day at a time to support me & my daughter, and to be as present and helpful to my parents as I could. The eldest daughter with divorce "shame." I was raised Catholic, and marriage was for life. I realize now that my parents were not in judgment. They were in quiet support for the rest of their lives. Mom quietly and dad slightly more verbose. They taught me about living in quiet entheos love to the best my ability.

I ask myself what stories I am telling myself about all parts of enthusiasm, synonyms, antonyms, and "full of God" message. Am I in the light, synonyms, or the lower energy, antonyms of enthusiasm. More to learn on both. I get to trust time to notice what stages of learning are available today. My bleak state of mind wants to keep me in the shadow. To block me from love's inner voice, the God within.

Over the years I have been blessed to let go of a few layers of shame around my divorce and walk in the light of self-love and self-discovery to the best of my ability with deep gratitude and enthusiasm. When I am truly "full of God," I can usually see my next steps to act or pause. The friend that I lost is now a gift in my life. Forgiveness and deep listening with Godly discernment assisted in healing this relationship.

I trust Divine timing with good intention letting go of forcing a situation. I notice what may be in the way. I am making my life my primary focus with self-discovery secondary with Godly discernment. All parts of my old patterns return in a new way. I get to remind myself to be aware and notice.

My hope is that the photo and my insights may assist you as you discover Love's Inner Voice, your relationship with YOU and others, and the enthusiasm within each connection. The light of love is a Divine gift of healing for me and one I love to share enthusiastically. I cherish the thought of being inspired and one with Divine loving energy and light.

Enthusiasm can be part of each day as we notice the beauty of life in a flower, laughter of a child, or the colors in the sky. It appears in how we feel, what we discover about ourselves and how we choose to show up each day. Divine energy, love and light are there when we are willing to listen and notice.

Imagine a world where we can see everyone as the light of divine energy. Awaken to Love's Inner Voice within you.

Be open to any questions specific to your journey.

PONDER & JOURNAL

* What feelings or thoughts have surfaced?

* Maybe judgment, anxiety/fear, a core belief, should?

* How does enthusiasm or entheos show up in my life?

* What changes do I wish to make?

* What or who may I need to truly listen to?

DISCOVERY IS VITAL

DISCOVER **SHOULD**

Many thoughts showed up when I saw this photo of me as I walked toward the Pacific Ocean at Salmon Creek. "I should" thoughts surfaced - I should have stood in a different place, I should be thinner, I should have noticed the sameness of the colors, I should be better than this at noticing before I take the photo. "If only" surfaced as well – if only I had a better camera, if only I had put my coat down so I did not look so big. Both low energy big time, which blocks out Love's Inner Voice, and "the God within," for me my soul.

You now know one of my challenges, my weight and body image. I worry about what others think I acknowledge when feelings about this show up, ask questions and turn them over to my God within Love's Inner Voice.

Louise Hay reminds me that "Is does not matter what other people say or do. What matters is what I chose to believe about myself."

SHOULD is the first word of the acronym for shame:

<u>S</u>hould <u>H</u>ave <u>A</u>lready <u>M</u>astered <u>E</u>verything
= SHAME

For me SHOULD and IF ONLY are encompassed in the acronym. A belief system that many of us may have.

Think about these words and notice what feelings or thoughts show up. Shame may knock with should. Be aware and notice what "guest" is knocking as Rumi reminds us. As soon as "should" knocks I ask, where is this coming from and what is there for me to learn. Usually, it reminds me to love and accept Brenda as I am in the moment.

"Before you speak ask yourself if what you are going to say is true, is kind, is necessary, is helpful. If the answer is no, maybe what you are about to say SHOULD be left unsaid."

—BERNARD MELTZER

SHOULD SYNONYMS – must, shall, will, allow, have to, ought to

SHOULD ANTONYMS – deny, reject, ignore, neglect

IF ONLY SYNONYMS – uncertainty, doubt, condition, assuming that

IF ONLY ANTONYMS – unless, except if, in spite of

"'IF ONLY' – lives in our past – it will always reside there – but how much room we allow it depends on us. We can allow those words to affect who we are now – for better or for worse."

—LOIS ASTWOOD

The Meltzer and Astwood quotes remind me to pause before I speak. Thus, how I respond to feelings and thoughts that show up are my choice. Do I want to show up as kind or a know-it-all? It is up to me and each of us as we walk through and with our life.

SHOULD and IF ONLY are usually safety, security, fear or judgment based.

I SHOULD have known...

You SHOULD do this...

I SHOULD... [**add your own**].

IF ONLY I had enough money.

IF ONLY I had more room.

IF ONLY I had a partner.

IF ONLY I had a loving family.

IF ONLY I had time.

IF ONLY... [**add your own**].

> **WHEN** – The other word that shows up many times with should and if only is "WHEN" related to feelings, judgment, not good enough and the like.
>
> **WHEN** SYNONYMS – allowing that, as long as it is, provided that
>
> **WHEN** ANTONYMS – before, prior to, after[3]

WHEN is usually more about control and unrealistic expectations with doubt, unworthiness, and fear participating. WHEN tends to focus on the outcome no matter what may be in the way.

---

3   *Thesaurus.com & Google*

WHEN I complete my masters, I will...

WHEN my partner gets better paying work, I will be happier.

WHEN I lose 50 pounds I will...

What have you experienced with WHEN? What feelings and thoughts come with "provided that..." – future-focused expectations.

Being the eldest of seven siblings, "have to" and "must" were part of our training for how to behave. This led to SHOULD and IF ONLY thinking for me when told: "watch out for your little brothers and sisters," "you are singing too loud," or laughing too loud," "there is nothing to cry about," and the like. I was and am emotional, especially when touched by beauty, kindness, music, family fun, and being seen—the tears flow.

Being teased for showing my emotions did not help. I remember going to my grandmother crying about being teased by the neighbor boys. Her comment was, "That is their way of showing they like you..." [One definition of teasing at thesaurus.com]. I did not believe her, as it hurt too much to be true. What showed was uncertainty and doubt or, IF ONLY. It felt uncaring because the teasers usually laughed after what they said, and they made sure no one was around. I never talked to her about my emotions again.

This experience supported my need to hide my feelings and take care of myself. To this day, it is hard to ask for help, especially when "doubt" and "ought to" show up. Remembering to ask, "Is it true?" "What help is needed?" and then listen feels out of reach at times. It comes faster with continuous practice. I consciously pay attention and surrender to what needs to be heard.

"If someone corrects you, and you feel offended, YOU have an EGO problem."

—NAUMAN ALI KHAN

"Everybody eventually surrenders to something or someone. If not to God, you will surrender to the opinions or expectations of others, to money, to resentment, to fear, or to your own pride, lusts, or ego."

—RICK WARREN

Ego does have a place in our lives. It is the gift of free choice when it comes from a heart place. I call it "little ego vs big EGO." They are both part of being human. It is up to me and all of us which one we want to base our decisions and choices on. Little ego allows us to notice others, big EGO rarely does in my experience. Who are you allowing to drive your bus?

Throughout my own discovery journey, I've come to realize that every time I think, say, or hear the word "should," "if only," or "when I'm usually sitting in "not good enough" or I'm moving into shame, an unrealistic expectation, fear or EGO.

EGO is "<u>E</u>dging <u>G</u>od <u>O</u>ut." For me it is blocking Love's Inner Voice because I'm focused on looking good, showing up in the "right" way or... [**add your own**], instead of deeply listening in present time.

"The EGO seeks to divide and separate. Spirit seeks to unify and heal."

—PEMA CHÖDRÖN

My dream for each day of my life to walk in the light and love of "entheos" to "unify and "heal" as Pema says. I have found that when I get out of my own way, I walk in the sunlight of love and am able to more easily identify my feelings and learn from "who" may be showing up.

I want to address fear or <u>F</u>alse <u>E</u>vidence <u>A</u>ppearing <u>R</u>eal = FEAR as it is a player with SHOULD, IF ONLY, WHEN and EGO. It may show up as doubt, not good enough, wanting more, or... [**add your own**].

Fear is an emotion we are given as part of our energetic make-up, a way to shine light on potential unsafe situation. When we choose not to notice it or say hello to it, fear can run amuck, especially if there is no bodily harm happening in that moment. What is the source of my fear? My little girl, teen, or. . .? What does this fear have to say? Listen deeply.

Feelings that may show up related to fear are not good enough, unworthy, lack, guilt, panic, and shame. Also, judgment, doubt, anxiety, loss, or resentment, and more. Anger may also raise its head after high stress situations. What emotions or feelings show up for YOU? Notice how the feelings can support you by asking you to pay attention or "drive your bus" until you do. There are no time limits or expectations not set by you. Emotions are gifts to support you on your unique life journey.

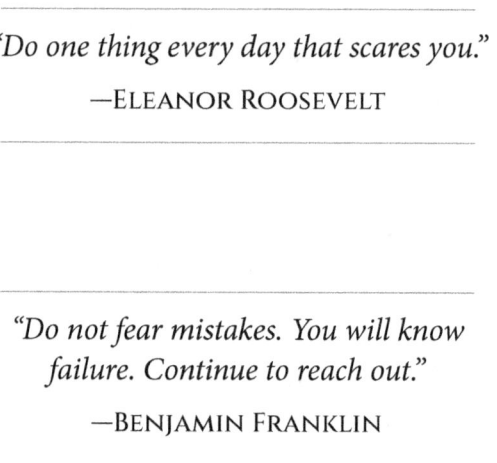

"Do one thing every day that scares you."

—ELEANOR ROOSEVELT

*"Do not fear mistakes. You will know
failure. Continue to reach out."*

—BENJAMIN FRANKLIN

Each quote shines light on aspects of being human. I make mistakes, that does not mean I am a mistake. Something a core belief may want me to believe to hide and stay safe.

All I have shared has the potential to block or open each of us from or to our sacred connection, love, experience compassion, acceptance, awareness, and more. You might also notice your energy level when these or like feelings or thoughts show up. How do they affect your body? What core beliefs are speaking or showing up?

I began to pay attention to my core beliefs (more in the next chapter) related to SHOULD, IF ONLY, and WHEN in my mid-60s. I continue to transform with the willingness to listen, learn and become a more authentic Brenda with a profound sacred connection, and increasing self-love. I also realized that I needed to choose to let go of what I call "big EGO," "Edging God Out" each day. For me, "little ego" (small letters) is a gift from the Divine, "my free choice" to walk in sacred connection and love's light. Kalil Gibran says it so well.

"Your living is determined not so much by what life brings to you as by the attitude you bring to life; not so much by what happens to you as by the way your mind looks at what happens."

—KHALIL GIBRAN

PONDER & JOURNAL

* Listen, notice, then take appropriate action. Document - write, draw, doodle, use non-dominant hand, or. . .

* How do should, if only, when, and EGO show up in my life?

* Notice when EGO might be driving me.

* Notice how often I think, say or hear "should," "if only, "when" and notice my reaction.

* Check out my subconscious about "should" by writing, drawing or. . . with my non dominant hand.

Pacific Ocean California

DISCOVER RELEASE

"I am sorry – Please forgive me Thank you – I love you."

—HO O PONO PONO – HAWAIIAN PRAYER

I love this prayer. I say it to myself or my body when I remember. I love that it has all the major elements – amends, forgiveness, gratitude, and love. Another prayer that speaks deeply to me is the Serenity Prayer. Both assist me to release or let go. Authors unknow for both prayers.

---

*"God, grant me the serenity to accept the things
I cannot change, courage to change the things I
can, and wisdom to know the difference."*

I chose the photo above as I saw, and experienced with her at the time, our response to the release of rainy-grey weather and experiencing enthusiasm and "entheos." Ho O Pono Pono and Serenity Prayer assist my release and discovery journey.

RELEASE SYNONYMS – let go, liberate, freedom, deliverance, surrender

RELEASE ANTONYMS – restraint, hold, check, inhibit, control

I find that each time I am willing to let go of a belief or feeling that no longer work for me is a gift. It gives me a chance to learn more about what is clogging connection to my Love's Inner voice. When I ask, pray, notice, and bring in gratitude, anything is possible, and releasing is easier.

Sometimes "let go" works better for me than release. Find what works for you. It is imperative for me to be aware if one of the antonyms show up, what some call "the shadow side" of our beingness. For me they show up as doubt to inhibit love related action, or restraint.

When my husband asked for a divorce and left me with a five-year-old, I experienced doubt, fear, abandonment, grief and pain. I was not as conscious of my inner voice of love as I am now. I did have to release him and trust that all would be well. I was gifted with at least two opportunities to let go and walk in faith that all would be well. For more of my story read my chapter in *Sacred Connection-Finding Our Path to Deeper Connection with Self and the Divine* an anthology by seven amazing women or keep reading.

I realized after a time that his leaving was a gift for us both. Our paths changed and yes, we had opportunities we may not have had, and some challenges too. I cannot say it enough; every challenge or life change is an opportunity to grow and expand my heart of love. The pain, challenge of letting go, and ongoing discovery is worth doing for my good, our good, and the highest good of all. I also realized that I could learn from and possibly transform the feelings that show up, or at least acknowledge them and then respond with love, compassion, or kindness.

I hope for freedom from pain and yet I cannot do it alone. I need "entheos," to be filled with God, and others to assist. Pain, grief [a later chapter], or suffering can be physical, emotional, psychological, or spiritual. All have played a different role in my life. You may wish to identify the pain in your life.

"I am arriving at the circle where one works on oneself as a gift to other people so that one doesn't create more suffering. I help people as I work on myself, and I work on myself to help people."

—RAM DASS

The last sentence of this quote speaks to me deeply. For me it's about honoring the insights I receive from others that can assist me to deepen my self-discovery to be more present for others. I like this kind of circle because it shows ongoing life, love, light and self-discovery opportunities.

This is how I say the Serenity prayer for today.

God, please grant me the serenity to accept all that I cannot change

The courage and willingness to change all that I can with You

And Your wisdom to know and accept the difference.

I encourage you to make any prayer, devotional, or affirmation your own. When I do that, all of me hears it, mind, body, spirit, emotions, and parts I may not yet be aware of. To me, that is miraculous. Doing this seems to make it easier for me to release stubborn beliefs, at least the story that I'm willing to let go. It can always be brought back if we wish.

I have noticed that my addictive thinking, or behaviors, may allow any behavior, feeling, or way of thinking to return sooner than later although probably not as strong. For me any repetitive thought, or behavior that does not serve me in my self-discovery journey may be an issue and addictive. Many come from core beliefs. This realization encourages me to look deeper.

Core beliefs fascinate me because I have found that many times, they play a role in my disconnect from Divine source, or entheos. My research took me to the Medical News Review[4] where I learned about CBT or Core Belief Therapy. The three-paragraph quote is from the website, updated February 11, 2025. The information in the quote speaks to my experience with some of my and many friend's core beliefs – the possible triggers that we have "no clue where that came from" experience.

"Core beliefs are deeply held beliefs that inform how people see themselves and the world. They have a large influence on people's perceptions and decision making.

"Core beliefs can be helpful, unhelpful, or neutral. Unhelpful or unrealistic core beliefs may negatively affect a person's mental health and overall life satisfaction.

"However, because core beliefs form such a large part of a person's worldview, a person may find it difficult to identify them. It also takes time and effort to change core beliefs."

—MEDICAL NEWS REVIEW

When I am willing to ask tough questions, especially when feelings surface, I can usually begin to get to a core belief. The amygdala, in the medial temporal lobe of the brain, processes feelings, particularly pain and anxiety. It has no words. The words come from the part of me that experienced the feeling and created the belief around it.

Core beliefs play a fairly large role in how we respond to life. When we are aware of their existence we can pause, ask for Godly discernment, listen, act and release if indicated. For me this is part of my discovery journey that

---

4   *See Appendix.*

is vital to enhance Love's Inner Voice. You may see more about them later as you continue your journey through this book and your life.

PONDER & JOURNAL

How might you utilize the prayers today? They are a great start to any amends you may choose to make. Release to the "God within" as you experience your Love's Inner Voice and express your joy as my beautiful friend is in the above photo. Awaken and let go.

Really look at how you respond on ALL level to the words of any prayer or affirmation. Look at the potential triggering words like forgive, can't, change, sorry, courage, and willingness to name a few. Some raise my interest, and I ask why, is there something here for me to learn, surrender, or transform?

* Am I ready to identify what no longer works for me and be willing to release or transform it?

* Do I have faith and trust that when I let go, something even better may show up? Be patient and listen.

* What part of me is having difficulty?

* What feelings have come up that I may want to say "hello" to and be curious about?

* How might I identify and transform or release core beliefs?

* What words or concepts trigger me?

DISCOVERY IS VITAL

Puget Sound Washington

DISCOVER
COMPLACENCY

*"Don't let your success of today lay you into complacency
for tomorrow. For that is the worst form of failure."*

—OG MANDINO

COMPLACENCY – self-satisfaction especially when accompanied by un-awareness of actual dangers or deficiencies.[5]

For me, and many of us, "failure" may not be an option. The word brings up not worthy or not good enough and feels big and heavy. What I have realized in my journey so far is that "failure" is a word that I can choose to believe or not. Am I willing to make a "mistake" into a glad to share it without thinking I am a failure.

5   *Marriam-Webster Dictionary*

These quotes remind me that it may not be in my best interest to rest on my laurels or be unaware. Action speaks louder than words. What action am I willing to take today to be of service to others. Words are great for auditory learners, pictures for visual learners and action, something physical, for kinesthetic learners.

I mention these brain function learning styles we are born with to encourage you to find out what journalling process may work best for you to move out of complacency. We each have all of them. I am primarily kinesthetic with visual and auditory equal much less. For example, it is important to me to be warm and comfortable with water close by when I am writing or in a zoom meeting. Many times, I paint my feelings on canvas.

> COMPLACENCY SYNONYMS – smugness, pride, laxness self-satisfaction, triumph, unawareness
>
> COMPLACENCY ANTONYMS – troubled, humble, humility, concerned, diffidence, self-doubt

I had a few discussions about keeping this word or changing it to a totally different word. After doing my research into definitions and synonyms as well as quotes, I believe it is "vital" that we all identify when we may be resting on our success or walking in self-doubt. One of the hardest questions I ask myself; "What lengths are you willing to go to change?"

As I reviewed the synonyms, I realized it is easy to feel smug, prideful, self-satisfied or... [add your own] to my and others detriment. My hope is that I pause long enough to ask myself, are any of these responses' kind, compassionate or loving. Probably not. What now? Move into the antonyms of humility or concerned and notice if troubled or self-doubt are speaking. Listen then take indicated action.

"Never settle in the comfort of complacency:
greatness awaits beyond."

—LUMINOUSQUOTES.COM

It's about being willing and curious when I feel complacent and figuring out what I choose to do to evaluate what I may wish to change. It is up to me. Asking my God within for assistance helps often by encouraging me to be honest with myself. This is one of my challenges sometimes. It can be hard to be brutally honest about the reasons or rationalizations I have for my choices. I hope to walk with "entheos" in the greatness of being present and loving no matter what is happening.

As a child, I developed a self-soothing habit of stuffing down my feelings with food and hiding in my room. The food was sweet or salty. I felt like I had to hide my feelings as I was teased, especially for tears or loud laughter.

I had three surgeries between five and six years of age. Parents were not allowed to stay with children in the mid-1950s. Visits were short, and sweets were usually included as a gift.

When we had a fall or small injury we were given a cookie or graham cracker – a sweet to sooth. An aspect of complacency for me is how I "feed" my challenges. As an emotional eater who attempts to honor and learn from my feelings and emotions, some days are a challenge. When I am stuffing down my feelings with food, food or the feeling is driving the bus. In my experience, others may choose to over exercise, shop, gamble, drink, or... [add your own].

For me it's about how I use my time to enhance and support Love's Inner Voice, my "God within." What am I thinking? How much time do I participate in distractions or rationalizations that raise their head to keep me in complacency. What or who is holding me back? Am I really that unaware? All questions writing about complacency bring up for me again. I realize I have a great "forgetter" especially of tough questions. Reminders are wonderful gifts that encourage awareness of my silent killers. Many in my experience; habits, thinking, patterns.

"Complacency is the silent killer of progress."

— LUMINOUSQUOTES.COM

Each day is a new day for self-discovery and deepening my connection to my loving inner voice. How can I show up as my true authentic self for myself or others when pride or thinking I know better may be "driving my bus" [me]? I can put on a good show. Is that how I wish to show up? Is that honest? I think not. What am I going to choose to do about it? Oh boy, yet more questions and more gifts to learn from and dismantle complacency today.

My dream is to be the best I can be each day for my good, our good, and the highest good of all. Sometimes, it's easy for me to be complacent, sitting in fear of failure, not good enough, or pride as I do sometimes. I need to let go of complacency to BE that dream. Challenges are gifts to learn and expand who Brenda is. When I walk in gratitude with my "God within" it's much easier.

"To grow, you must confront the comfort of complacency."

—LUMINOUSQUOTES.COM

There are many illuminating quotes pertaining to complacency. This one reminds me that I have a choice to "confront" my addictive or unhealthy behaviors or remain in complacency of which I may be unaware. I am less likely to be oblivious when I am "filled with God." No one ever said that growth would be comfortable. The question for me is always "Am I willing to go at any length to let go or transform my addictive behaviors that lead to complacency?" It is about trusting the process and faith for the result with the ongoing support of "Love's Inner Voice."

I let the questions be an opportunity to "confront the comfort of complacency." Awaken Love's Inner Voice as I notice when I am complacent, sitting on my success or possible unawareness. I get to experience bravery when listening to my feelings and notice how they show up in my mind, body, and spirit. It is truly about how I wish to show up in the world. How much I am willing to love and accept who I am today. How do I respond to feelings and life challenges. My wish is to honor who I am, especially the gift of life we have all been given. My reminder: notice, awaken, discover, expand.

PONDER & JOURNAL

* How is complacency showing up in my life?

* What thoughts, beliefs or behavior distract me or "drive my bus"?

* What questions or emotions show up?

* What lengths am I willing to take to move out of complacency?

* What iterations of complacency show up in my life?

Face Rock, Oregon USA

DISCOVER **ACCEPTANCE**

*"Acceptance of what has happened is the first step to
overcome the consequences of any misfortune."*

—WILLIAM JAMES

This quote is about choosing how I wish to respond to challenges or misfortunes that show up. Acceptance has MANY definitions. I chose two sentences that support Love's Inner Voice message.

ACCEPTANCE – "An acceptance of someone or something is also an indication that you approve of or believe in it (or them)." "A disposition to tolerate or accept people or situations."[6]

The picture of Face Rock reminds me of the calm of meditation or being in the moment with the waves of life flowing around and over me. She is

6   Vocabulary.com

steady no matter how big the waves are. Sitting and experiencing the magic of this giant rock that Mother Earth created calms me into acceptance of all I have to offer, and various choices I get to make. My unique perspective of how to flow with life in a dance with "entheos" for my good, our good, and the highest good of all.

I have had some resistance to the word "work." A friend asked me why I didn't use the word job. She then shared the acronym she created Joy of Being = **JOB**. Oh my, absolutely. That is my, our, JOB as spirits in a body here on earth in my brain's opinion. It makes writing, necessary paperwork so much smoother. For me, when I am in the joy and light of Love's Inner Voice, the job flows as the water flows over Face Rock in the now.

Some challenges for me at times, is to accept Brenda's emotions, addictive behaviors, tears, and physical issues with love and compassion. If I am unable to do that, how am I able to accept others as they are? It really is about accepting "I am that, I am" a 3500-year-old mantra of my soul known as "The Moses Code" by James E Twyman. God is known by many as the great I AM. When I say "I am that, I am" I am accepting my challenges in the moment. It's like a breath of fresh air. This assists me to be aware of who or what is driving my bus in the moment.

What can I do to move me back into love's light? Pause, heart breathe, doodle my emotions, and ask what or who needs attention currently? I choose to act with Love's Inner Voice. Dustin Lance Black says it well, "If you do something with acceptance and kindness, you can create a true friendship," with Brenda and others.

What I really may need to ask myself; "Is there anything here I need to surrender, or am I in resistance?" I can then get creative based on the answer. If surrender, I review; is there anything to learn or is it about change, transformation, or let go. If I have a resistant feeling, from where or whom and do I have any control of what I am resistant to. Or do I need to move into surrender? It is interesting how synonyms and antonyms have a role to play in our lives. They can be a gift of recognition or a challenge. Life's wave action.

ACCEPTANCE SYNONYMS – receptiveness, surrender, receptivity

ACCEPTANCE ANTONYMS – resistance, defiance

Acceptance of what I cannot change is a challenge for me some days. I love the *Serenity Prayer*. It reminds me to look at what I can change and accept what I cannot change or control. The primary thing I can control every day is how I choose to respond to life situations and to be open to be God filled. I choose to look at what I can control and what I cannot and think I can. What story might I be telling myself to "think I can?"

Some days I struggle with the belief that I can care for everyone and keep them safe, right? As the eldest of seven siblings, from the time I was nine or ten-years-old, every time I left the house I heard "watch out for your younger brothers and sisters." Yes, this is a story I tell myself and it is true to the best of my recollection. For me it was about making sure they were safe. In essence being "mom," which one of my sisters later in life told me I was not. For me, I was doing as I was told.

At age 11, I was babysitting for families with four to seven children in the neighborhood. That summer, I was asked to fly from Seattle to Lompoc California to assist one of my aunts with who just had her seventh child in six and a half years, no twins. Luckily, I had an uncle with a small Cessna and was willing to fly me down and back. I loved it because he let me fly the plane for a short time. Caring for and about others became ingrained. No wonder I became an RN. More caregiving.

"Tolerance, compromise, understanding, acceptance, patience – I want those all to be very sharp tools in my shed."

—CEELO GREEN

Living life with these attributes, a gift of being truly present. After all, isn't that my job: joy of being? Yes, no matter what challenges show up. Acceptance of what "is," that I cannot change, is part of life's ebb and flow.

I still ask for patience although not as much as I used to. I realized that the more I asked for patience, the more opportunities I was given to practice patience. I noticed how often I receive learning opportunities for what I ask for. How many times have I been upset about how often I have these opportunities and think "I asked for patience, why do I not have any?" A life paradox. Life is full of them in my experience.

Rigorous honesty with myself is one of the hardest things for me to do. I am very good at talking "story" and rationalizing to myself. How does that serve me or anyone else? Listening to Love's Inner Voice is about deep honesty and acceptance of the sacred Brenda...[**add your name**] today. This takes energy, determination and acceptance.

"Acceptance looks like a passive state, but, in reality, it brings something entirely new into this world. That peace, a subtle energy vibration, is consciousness."

—ECKHART TOILE

PONDER & JOURNAL

* How does acceptance or resistance show up in my life?

* When resistance show up, what is my initial response? How do I handle my response?

* What do I have no control over?

* What am I having difficulty surrendering?

* Am I willing to walk in humility to acceptance? If not, why not?

Pacific Ocean California

DISCOVER **FORGIVENESS**

This photo depicts the potential paths of my forgiveness choices. The sand of indecision, never stable, the beauty of nature rooted in the sand showing me that when I'm willing to walk in forgiveness I also have stability. The shadow, refusal to shine light on my feelings and discover the cause. When I pause and feel unforgiveness I can better choose how I wish to respond in the NOW.

FORGIVENESS SYNONYMS – pardon, amnesty, mercy, clemency

FORGIVENESS ANTONYMS – retribution, chastise, condemnation

"Just knowing you don't have all the answers is a recipe for humility, openness, acceptance, forgiveness, and an eagerness to learn – and those are all good things."

—DICK VAN DYKE

This quote speaks to my heart. How am I able to forgive or accept anyone if I am feeling a need for retribution or chastising for unkindness or... [**add your own**].

The other phase that challenges me is "knowing you don't have all the answers." With all my experience, there are many times I think I do. Then I realize that I am a guide only, we all get to find and learn our own answers. Acknowledging that I do not have all the answers truly is living in humility and honesty.

I also realized walking this forgiveness path is that I really cannot forgive anyone who has not asked for forgiveness. An interesting paradox when thinking about childhood trauma related to a parent or guardian. All I can do is accept that the parent's own pain and trauma created unconsciousness of the behavior. This can be hard for trauma survivors to accept. It truly is about believing in me and my worthiness of goodness and love, after all, God loves me unconditionally.

When I'm feeling the need to chastise, am I not being unkind? "Eagerness to learn" from the quote encourages me to continue to ask the hard questions, pause and listen. If I am willing to learn from my feelings, emotions, challenges, mistakes and more, I am willing to be the best I can be today, and I've opened myself to Love's Inner Voice. The path of forgiveness can't change the past. We all have a choice whether to walk in the light or dark of forgiveness.

The light "I forgive you" or "Please forgive me" with no expectations. Where may this lead – learning, conversation, acceptance, and healing. This allows me to make mistakes too and forgive myself for being human. A gift of light – it's OK to be an imperfect human.

The dark "I'll never forgive you." Heavy energy may lead to – loss, grief, or loneliness. I am capable of wallowing in "why me" and the like. I am better at identifying it faster and moving out of it.

Have you ever said or felt either? What happened? Do you always have to be perfect? The gift of darkness, a path to recovery and discovery when I am willing.

My ex-husband, whom I married in 1975, did not ask me for forgiveness. I am not sure he could do so at the time. I forgave myself for my part in the relationship. I did many things that were not in my ethics to keep us together. He in turn brought home diseases to me. I did not have the awareness then, that I have today. It was a deep learning time for me. It took me time to accept that he was walking in deep Vietnam pain, anger and PTSD, especially related to experiencing friendly fire deaths of comrades. Feelings running amuck. His anger and pain put holes in hollow core doors. No physical harm to me and our daughter. Emotional and psychological harm to me, realized many years later.

Despite obtaining a bachelor's degree in nursing in 1971, the program did not address emotional eating or how to deal with emotions in a healthy way. We spent time in a VA hospital with Vietnam vets before PTSD was identified, during our psychology rotation. It was heartbreaking for me to see young men my age walking around in an emotional fog, not sure who they were, what was next, and in panic with any loud noise. My emotions were triggered during this time. I had difficulty being with them and yet wanted to comfort them at the same time. I received no support from my instructor and received a low grade due to my response to the experience. It was not OK to show emotion. For her, it was all about the mind.

I lived in my emotions and feelings for years after both experiences. I ate sweet and salty things to stuff my feelings down to a reasonable level. I thought that was the best thing to do to show up for my daughter after the divorce in 1981. She was five years old. I have apologized to my daughter for various upheavals in her life. She accepts me with love and kindness.

I have learned to do, in many situations, as Lily Tomlin recommends "For fast acting relief, try slowing down." It is about pausing to breath, notice what I'm feeling and choosing how I wish to show up in that moment.

When I pause it is an action of clemency for me. The conscious breath also brings me more easily into congruence with my heart and Love's Inner Voice.

When I choose to feel the need to condemn or chastise myself or others, I am usually walking in unforgiveness. This lowers my energy and rarely supports spiritual, energetic, emotional or physical healing. Noticing how I'm being in the moment is typically opens me to recovery and God awareness. Healing can be accomplished by using many modalities.

Modalities I use are Reiki, tapping [EFT], havening, writing, sharing with a like-minded person, prayer, reading, painting, and exercise to name a few. It's about noticing what works for me at any given moment and being willing to choose me next step.

Asking for assistance from spirit or human may be hard at times. I find that the harder it feels the more I need to let go of control and walk in willingness and surrender. I have found this becomes easier with practice. Walking in forgiveness is about being willing to learn and possibly change my perspective for the greater good of all. Life continually reminds me that change is inevitable like the waves of the ocean. I get to choose whether to flow with it or resist it. Life doesn't care. It's beneficial for me to notice what I care about and why.

PONDER & JOURNAL

* What feelings arise when I think about forgiveness?

* Is it difficult for me to forgive and love me? When? Why?

* What is difficult about loving and accepting myself as I am today?

* What gets in the way of me accepting others as they are?

Lake Tahoe California

DISCOVER **TRUST**

The beauty of the photo and the quote remind me to slow down, notice, and feel the energy around me. I can trust Mother Nature to support me as we are a part of each other. I may not understand all that happens and I trust it is for the greatest good of earth and us. All created by "entheos" energy, a part of me and trust.

I ended the chapter on forgiveness with this belief, "It's beneficial for me to notice what I care about and why." I have learned to trust my Love's Inner Voice, a benefit to the way I chose to live and be present for others. Is it easy all the time? There are frequent challenges on any path I choose. It remains my choice.

I also chose the quote and photo to remind me that nature trusts me and all of us to care about and for "her." I trust that there is healthy food to eat, air to breathe, and water to drink.

> **TRUST** SYNONYMS – faith, rely on, believe, confidence, confide
>
> **TRUST** ANTONYMS – keep, withhold, doubt, discredit, suspect

Being honest with myself and others is the basis for trust in my experience and as Albert Einstein says, "Whoever is careless with the truth in small matters cannot be trusted with important matters."

The small "white lies" I have told in the past to look or sound good are a disservice to me and others. When I look back, I notice how low my energy was. It's so easy to do when I feel unworthy in any way. If I cannot be honest with myself, how can I be truly honest with others. It is so important to be honest with those I love and trust. Many times, I choose to ask for spiritual guidance. I realize how little I really know and remember when I read authors like Emerson.

> *"All I have seen teaches me to trust the Creator for all I have not seen."*
>
> —RALPH WALDO EMERSON

Much as I wish to believe I can control situations in which I feel uncomfortable, in fear, or doubt, when I'm honest, I know I cannot. It can be hard to admit to others I need help or am unable to complete a task as created. This attitude of acceptance and sharing supports trust, faith, and confidence within me and in my relationships.

In a meeting I was in today, the word vigilance came up. I realized that to build trust in myself and others, being vigilant about body language, tone of voice, honesty, and words used is vital to nurture trust and authenticity. Like anything else, I can take this into being controlling or perfectionism, not of service to anyone. I have found that neither foster trust nor self-love.

They do give me an opportunity for deeper self-discovery, sometimes a challenge.

I notice when my mind is encouraging me to withhold or suspect information and my feelings. I have experienced so much false energy, fraud, and dishonesty recently and in my nursing career. So many may be walking in fear for their life or family well-being. It can be very scary and intimidating for many.

"Never be afraid to trust an unknown future to a known God."

—CORRIE TEN BOOM

Twice in my nursing career I lived in this quote. My daughter was ten years old, we were living in San Francisco in a condo I bought with my parents' assistance. I was asked to leave a job in a hospital after four years because I "was not doing my share of the work." I was a head nurse of a medical unit, involving staffing, utilization review, and total care for at least two patients every day. I did not believe I was informed of the true underlying reason I was asked to leave or be fired. I chose to leave so I would receive a good recommendation.

I was without a job for three months and in fear, on food stamps, living on my savings, job hunting and being as calm as I was able to for my daughter, and yet being as honest as I could. I was an emotional wreck and eating emotionally, believing that would help. The Creator took care of us when I asked and found me a job as an educator in a long-term care facility. Eight months later, I was headhunted for an assistant director of nursing position over three long term care units and the Infection Control program for the nine-unit facility. Another road in my nursing career I had not thought of exploring. Listening to Love's Inner Voice, my connection to a loving energy, assists me in ways I cannot see as Emerson and Boom have shared. They also remind me that all I have is the present moment to be the best I can be, kind, trustworthy, and compassionate for myself and others.

One of the hardest challenges around trust I've experienced is trusting my thinking about what will help my emotions when I forget to ask the God within for assistance. My mind tells me that I can take care of this, don't take up God's time.

PAUSE = Perhaps Another Unseen Solution Exists

Stuffing them down with any addictive behavior does not work and strengthens my addictive thinking. Pausing to take conscious breath, or drink of water usually brings me into the now so I can question what is happening, who's "driving my bus" and is that my choice? This is one of the ways I train my thinking and myself to pause and ask.

What addictive behaviors show up in my life? Emotional eating which I work on every day with God. TV watching movies, mysteries, documentaries, and travel. Reading and playing games on my kindle can take up a lot of time as well as looking at my photos and thoughts of unworthiness come in more than I would like.

Trust brings many feelings for most beings. Be open to what or who shows up to deepen your sacred awakening of Love's Inner Voice. Mother Nature trusts each of us to care about our planet and each other. The earth cares for us when we show up and do our part for her and others.

PONDER & JOURNAL

* What addictive thoughts or behaviors may stifle trust?

* Do I trust an outside loving energy, to care about me?

* Who/what do I really trust?

* Do I trust my inner knowing, soul, or intuition?

* Am I worthy of trust?

* What feelings showed up? Do I trust them? Why or why not?

* What role do I choose to play related to trust and other beings on our loving planet?

Bodega Head – Pacific Ocean California

DISCOVER JUDGMENT

When you look at the picture chosen to represent judgment, what thoughts or feelings came to visit? I chose this photo for judgment because it's a lovely place I've experienced many times with the two friends pictured. Connection to nature in a deep encompassing way assists me to be more connected to a higher frequency of energy.

When I like or dislike something, it is still a judgment that I may wish to investigate with curiosity. Curiosity has a much higher vibration than "why me" or "not again." It's easier for me to integrate any message being shared.

JUDGMENT SYNONYMS – verdict, opinion, decision, belief

JUDGMENT ANTONYMS – fact, truth

Do I have any right to judge anyone or anything at any time? If I believe I do, who gives mt the right? Probably my ego.

If I judge I better be ready to be judged. Only my creator judges from a place of love and acceptance, and yet I am my worst critic of being unworthy of such love.

I may judge many experiences or what I see based on feelings or background. Is that fair to a person or situation? Judging someone or something can lead to resentment, anger, anxiety, fear, and always decreased loving energy. I am then closed off from what is present to teach me. My wish is to notice my feelings or thoughts and experience the gift of choice about my response and a chance to increase self-awareness and vital energy frequency.

My first exposure to 12-step spiritual principles was in July 2016, a gift and a challenge at the same time. I have an issue with sugar and dessert carbs. I was raised Catholic; thus, I knew their definition of "God." Even as a young child I knew there was a kinder, and loving energy. Sin is one of the things talked about frequently as a heavy burden when unconfessed. It can be the way I was taught for 20 years. The biggest burden I carry today is self-judgment.

Honesty is the first spiritual principle in any 12-step program. One of the hardest daily practices for me many days. Honest with myself about what I'm eating, even more about what feelings and thoughts may show up to set up a detour or roadblock from my fullness of God.

I was encouraged by my Higher Power and a mentor to write my first "Discovery is" book. Being an author was never on my radar. I was a nurse and a caregiver, not an author.

"No one can make you feel inferior without your consent."

—ELEANOR ROOSEVELT

The Eleanor Roosevelt quote reminds me that blaming someone else, or a situation for how I feel does not serve me or anyone else. I strive to be curious about what triggered my feelings or emotions [**add your own**] to learn and possibly surrender a belief or opinion. Many times it's about cleaning out my thinking, core beliefs, and energy.

An opinion is not fact and has gotten me in challenging situations where I believed I was right and later found to be incorrect. Accepting the mistakes I make is a gift as well. It is part of being a uniquely imperfect human "be-ing." That is my job; to be the best I am able in the NOW and let worry [past focused], or fear [future focused] go.

Yet another reminder to ask myself when feelings come up, are they future or past focused and what do I choose to do next

More difficult when I am in doing instead of being, which is much of the time. That is OK as there is much to do. My prayer is that I am doing as much as possible awake in conscious choice. So many times I am in automatic mode, oblivious of what is happening around me or even bodily needs.

What do I truly wish to cultivate in my energetic garden of love and light? For me, that is what Love's Inner Voice nurtures. I do that with random acts of kindness, a heartfelt smile, a hug, or showing up as my genuine human self. There are many ways to shine my light. It is not about being the star on the stage. It is about being quietly of service, quietly and lovingly creating a meal, being a loving single mom, or showing up at work on time. I have mentioned many ways I have been of service. These are samples of energetic songs I sing. Add your own if you wish.

I accept and support that everyone has their own song to sing in this life. I wish to be sure mine is the one I choose to sing when I came into this life, uncolored by others or judgments learned. Living the fullness of Brenda each day no matter what comes.

As a kinesthetic, my primary brain preference, I learn most easily by touch and smell. Hugs are very important and yet I always ask before I hug anyone. Covid arrived. No more in person meetings with hugs, or hugging neighbors. I had to find other ways to fulfill this need. I started hugging trees, with their consent, especially a large oak tree I pass when I go for walks with a neighbor. I felt a return hug every time without judgment, my heart filled with love. I touch that beautiful being when I pass with gratitude for its support during challenging times.

Zoom, despite what many people think, has been a gift as well. Meeting and sharing with people all over the world is a gift. I receive loving energetic hugs at each meeting I attend. Self-hugs are a must. There are many ways to do that for me. More about that in another chapter.

I was gifted with a realization today that in certain circumstances I am hypervigilant which can easily lead to unashamedly judging someone or a situation. Taking notice of my environment, my body and energy are very informative. There have been times when I was blind to me and how I was responding. Even simple situations like putting a cover over my adult trike can be a challenge and has my whining "why is this happening?." The Serenity Prayers is full of reminders to let go and let God. My JOB is to walk in the Joy of Being whatever comes. Being in the moment, the emotions, the challenges and learn. Surrender any judgment that shows up.

"Blind and naked ignorance delivers brawling judgment, unashamed on all things all day long."

—ALFRED LORD TENNYSON

Many times, I remember putting my challenge in my cupped hands and notice how heavy it is, and any message revealed. I then rub my hands in slow motion, eyes closed and being with the energy. I do this a few times sensing, curious and open to the light of Love's Inner Voice. It's hard for me to be in "brawling judgement" as Tennyson says when I choose to walk in loves light and acceptance. The quote does remind me how easily I can be in that muck. As a dear friend, Ann Jonas, reminds me that I cannot blossom without the muck.

"For whatever reason we were put on this planet at this time together, and I think we're supposed to figure this out together. Every aspect of nature and every healthy ecosystem has that divergence."

—ADRIENNE MAREE BROWN

PONDER & JOURNAL

* What do I want to cultivate?

* When does judgment show up in my life?

* What does it feel like on all levels – spiritual, emotional, physical

* Is there anything I am curious about right now?

* Have I experience "brawling judgment" toward myself or others? Describe.

DISCOVERY IS VITAL

Pacific Ocean California

DISCOVER **BALANCE**

"Balance is not something you find; it's something you Create."

—JANA KINGSFORD

L ife balance is my creation in partnership with my intuition, emotions, mind and divine energy connection. I look at how many pieces of wood it took to create balance in the shelter, and all the footprints in the sand that blend and change in balance with nature. It seems like a little bit of magic.

BALANCE SYNONYMS – equilibrium, stability, steadiness, security

BALANCE ANTONYMS – unbalance, volatility. inconsistency, instability

Balance is a word I can get tired of hearing because many times I struggle to figure out what it looks like in real life. I feel like I'm in balance with a given situation and then change steps in. For me change many times leads to imbalance. Yet, I consider the times of change gifts to learn from. The balance paradox in action.

Paradox: dichotomy, enigma, or mystery are some of its synonyms. Maybe this chapter word could be paradox as could each focus word. I find that is true in my life. Many times, in my experience I was connected to mother earth and at the same time to my Divine knowingness. I cannot explain, it is a combination of knowing and feeling. A mystery to many and way of being for others.

I was listening to author, energy intuitive and channeler Lee Harris speak about his newest book *The Future Human* and having one foot in the earthly realm and the other in the spiritual future realm. I have been blessed to feel that way when I am reading energy or connecting with the divine. It feels balanced until I start thinking about it. I can feel doubt creeping in until I notice and do some conscious heart breathing bringing me back to my center.

Can life be balanced and unbalanced or any of the other antonyms at the same time? It seems so, at least in my experience. Does being in balance define me? No. Being honest about my experience and doing my best to walk in the light of love defines me to my toes. I experienced the same energy when the aurora borealis came into my life in 1973 and touched me down to my toes, being centered. The feeling of being centered shows up again when I see nature's beauty, while hugging a tree, do a Reiki healing, tapping [EFT][7], or Havening[7] to name a few.

What does paradox or the aurora have to do with balance you may be asking. Vitality or energy. For me it's energy, creativity, and dancing in the light and shadow within me.

How do I know if I am in balance. One of the best ways I have found is to write a list of my personal assets and challenges. I do this, not to compare, to notice where I spend most of my time and what there is for me to learn or change. Staying out of judgment as I do this assists balance.

---

7   *See Appendix.*

If I feel stuck and writing is no help, I love to doodle. I doodle white on black to see what wants to show up as well as the color on white with colored pencil or acrylic paint. I enjoy painting me feelings because I can add, change and label each with date and feeling as reminders that "this too shall pass" as the adage says.

Some emotions, feeling and thoughts that can shift me out of balance are not good enough, unworthy, fear of doing it wrong, perfectionism, thinking I must fix or "mother" those in pain, shame, dishonesty with myself, strong feelings of any kind, and more... [**add your own**].

Assets I have noticed are compassion, kindness, accepting, caring, agreeable, charitable, humble, intelligent, willing, positive, loyal, and more... [**add your own**].

Many times, when I feel uncertain or uncomfortable I ask myself "what is there here to discover" then notice what comes up... [**add your own question of curiosity**]. What fire am I willing to light to be the best I can be in any situation, even when experiencing a challenging issue or feeling? No one else can light my fire for discovery. It comes from the cosmic heart via Love's Inner Voice. Human and spirit together in a cosmic dance.

"You cannot, you cannot use someone else's fire. You can only use your own. And in order to do that, you must first be willing to believe that you have it."

—AUDRE LORDE

I have found Lorde's perspective to be true. There is only one unique me and thus my fire, path, way of being human currently is unique. Attempting to act in a way that is untrue to me keeps me from my own fire of authenticity and connection. I've noticed that the "invisible ceiling" or walls of my spiritual link changes depending on how honest, authentic, balanced and centered I am. Is that how I wish to define Brenda. I accept how Erin French says it. I really do not wish walls to define me, even though I feel like hiding from my feelings, thinking, or food cravings. Hiding is a wall from honesty and hope I've noticed as they are important for me to hear Love's Inner Voice.

"Walls had never defined me, like I had once thought.
It was what I brought, from my heart, hands, and
soul to the space within that defined me."

—ERIN FRENCH

Balance and being centered feel the same to me although, centered is more body spirit for me. Balance more mind feeling focused. Interesting, yet another paradox. Writing this book teaches more about me, who I am, how I respond to situations and how much I have yet to learn if I chose to do so. Enthusiasm lives in me when I notice the opportunities that show up for me to explore. I look forward to seeing what others have to say about their experience, their journey.

I am also learning to give myself hugs of love, acceptance, and comfort in many ways to knock down the walls I may have created. Some of the ways I do this are self-hugs, dancing around the house with my red maracas, drum or rhythm sticks, calling a friend, going for a walk, taking pictures of the beauty around me, heart breathing, and even doodling... [add your own]. All and more allows me to move into balance when I'm willing and to be open to my cosmic heart.

PONDER & JOURNAL

* What does balance have to share or create in me?

* What aspects of me stand in my way?

* What aspects of me assist me?

* What ceilings and walls do I create?

* What paradoxes do I notice in my life.

* What else is showing up around balance?

DISCOVER **CONNECTION**

"We are all connected to Mother Earth, the universe,
and each other. Honor and learn each day."

—BL BALDING

It really is all about NOW and how I am connected whether I acknowledge it or not. Each of us is part of nature with a beating heart, lungs breathing, eyes seeing, ears listening, body touching, and yet individually unique.

I changed the photo many times before I chose the connection the bee has with the orange blossom. Originally there was a photo of a group of people I traveled with in front of an Irish castle. In the original photo, there is only one person I remain connected to. We have been traveling buddies for about thirty years. By the time I arrived at this chapter, I realized I wanted to explore deeper connections.

CONNECTION SYNONYMS – affinity, relation, association, link

CONNECTION ANTONYMS – variance, incongruence, incompatible

Back to the bee and orange blossom. When I saw the orange tree with a few open blossoms, many closed, and a few bees hovering I had to take multiple photos. The affinity I felt with the beautiful aroma, the sound of the bees, the contrasting colors, and the thought of all the yummy oranges and honey was a gift on many levels. Notice all the connections and synchronicities in the adventure of me, the bee and the orange blossom. Simple and full at the same time. What other connections might I notice and possibly learn from?

"And then the day came, when the risk to remain tight in a bud was more painful than the risk it took to blossom."

—ANAÏS NIN

Reading this quote, I ask in what ways do I want to blossom? What links within me do I wish to make in addition to external associations? I hope to continue to connect with all parts of me that are sleeping currently. Affinity with others, nature, energy frequencies all assist me.

My bond and association with others add depth and breadth to my life and internal discovery.

What blossom am I unwilling to let bloom in me? I observe Mother Nature and take many pictures. Like the orange bud, to blossom, to fruit cycle, I get concerned that when I attempt to create something it will not be good enough and it may fade away, be too costly, or not as expected. Moving past this is the painful part that Anaïs Nin speaks of. Am I willing to trust the process, do my part and allow what I want to create to blossom? [**Are you?**]

I struggled with this question more with my first book than with this creation. My dream is that each person who reads this notices links and affinities they never dreamed possible. I know I have as I continue my Love's

Inner Voice discovery journey. I realize I connect with our world and all its beings, and energies on so many levels. Many I am unable to put into words. Feelings of awe, joy, wonder, and sometimes disbelief with all the beautiful beings I am connected to. My heat swells with love and acceptance.

Yes, there are usually challenges or painful parts along life's journey. I continue to have free choice about what action I take related to the challenges. What I wish to learn and what I wish to surrender. Surrender is part of the growth process as well. How many relationships have been severed due to circumstances that changed my life. More than I can count or remember. They are all still a part of who I am because of our connection.

I love the life metaphor of the balloon man walking around fairs with a large bunch of balloons. The center balloons represent me and my close connections. When a breeze comes up the balloons suddenly shift. Now some of the inner circle balloons have been replaced by ones from the outside. I now have new links and may continue contact with those who have moved away or not. New opportunities to grow and learn.

I live alone and have done so for the last thirty years or so. I have a "God within" connection most of the time. When I feel lost, stuck or... [**fill in the blank**], I find that I can connect with any of my spiritual family, and at times, my genetic family, for ease and comfort.

For me this means having links with neighbors who assist each other. I also attend zoom meetings, circles, and classes that feed my soul. Sharing my story in my unique way assists as well. And life is a story that I can choose to change any time. I ask myself, what stories are in me that continue to be a mystery and may be separating me from deeper affinities. Separation from Love's Inner Voice, my spiritual connection or even physical well-being. Mysteries to be discovered. Living life to its fullest today.

"For whatever reason we were put on this planet at this time together, and I think we're supposed to figure this out together. Every aspect of nature and every healthy ecosystem has that divergence."

—ADRIENNE MAREE BROWN

The quote reminds me that I am spirit in a human existence by choice. I am a divine feminine, divine masculine, and soul connected to all. Some people may call it trinity or synchronicity. I am energy in human form as I believe everyone is.

I am very grateful for all the wonderful connections I have been gifted with. Brown's quote encouraged me to appreciate the connections I have. If I can enhance my brain, so much the better. And willingness to continue to connect with all parts of me for my good and the greatest good of all. After all, my passion is to share my discoveries about Love's Inner Voice with anyone who wishes to listen and discover more about themselves. It's fun playing in the muck of life most of the time. The discovery may include connections I never even thought of. Accepting challenges may be the path to deep wisdom and joy.

I leave you with a prayer I appreciate. Notice what it may bring up as you read it.

"Guide my attention to that which is worthy of it: making art, cooking food, loving people, noticing birds, petting dogs, contacting friends, and doing the work that is mine to do."

—NADIA BOLZ-WEBER

PONDER & JOURNAL

* What work is mine to do?

* Why would I want to keep any experience or person away that may enhance love's inner voice awakening?

* What feelings show up for me?

* "Who has come to guide you today," Rumi reflects. Be open and discover.

* What is in my way of showing kindness and compassion to me?

* How am I honoring my connections today?

DISCOVERY IS VITAL

DISCOVER **GRIEF**

"If we don't allow ourselves the fundamental honesty of our own sadness, then we miss an important cue to adapt."

—KATHERINE MAY

I chose this photo because it represents nature's life, death, and rebirth process. We are of nature and experience the same in different ways. Let's look at each one separately.

LIFE – green leaves, the fading scent, being in the present moment

Life happens for me instead of to me even when I may not like it. If I Don't like it, questions I can ask. What have I created, where am I in my mind or beliefs, what story am I telling myself, or caging myself in? What do I want to commit to now or surrender? What story am I living? Is it mine or someone else's rules? Comparison is the death of joy or beauty. What am I willing to learn from nature? I have a choice to commit to being right or being the light of kindness and love. How I live my life is a choice. It's about "innerstanding" - what energy am I choosing to stand in right now? [**What energy are you experiencing right now?**]

> DEATH – loss of flower petals, last petal, shrinking petals

What I resist persists is a saying many have. I have experienced many losses, what I call mini deaths. I call them mini deaths when I do not acknowledge them and grieve them. Some might be as simple as someone not showing up at a scheduled meeting, or one I forget to show up for. How easy it is for me to move into feelings of "not good enough," or "I should have..." When I leave these feelings unnoticed, they fester and grow into shame, self-blame or more. "Death" of a sort because I'm shutting the door on a part of me that wants to be seen.

> REBIRTH – seed pod, pollen, roots

I do not want to miss a chance to adapt, transform, and grow within. I experience grief in my unique way as we all do. I am noticing that each time I think of my dad, I feel different about his recent passing. I wanted an anagram that supports my, and hopefully others, journey with the emotion of grief.

<u>G</u>rateful <u>R</u>ebirthing <u>I</u>nternal <u>E</u>nergy <u>F</u>low
= GRIEF

Yes, rebirthing who I am now as the eldest who does not want to be the family matriarch. When I am honest, no one asks me to be. The realization that my siblings and I are the elder generation in my immediate family. How do I want to show up now is my choice with the guidance of love's inner voice.

It took a healing trip to visit a friend in Hawaii to realize I needed to rebirth myself into Brenda NOW. I had been focusing some on me and much on my dad the last five years of his life (more about this in the next chapter).

Being in today is the only time I own to learn, discover, and listen. After all, it is my job to be the best I can be, not perfect, and yet perfectly uniquely

Brenda no matter what I am experiencing or feeling. I also realized that many circumstances and life experiences elicit the feeling of grief.

When I look at the grief synonyms, I realize how frequently grief can arise. I was surprised and grateful I could now name some of the feelings I.ve had and do have. I am now able to heal or release them as I learn from them.

GRIEF SYNONYMS – sorrow, guilt, anguish, remorse, pain, heartache

GRIEF ANTONYMS – joy, delight, extasy, pleasure, happiness

Most of us can list life happenings that lead to grief like, death, loss, trauma... [name yours]. I realized that I felt grief after the birth of my beautiful, lively daughter. It was the loss of closeness and deep connection as I nurtured her in my womb. The loss of her placenta was the finality of the loss. I was in tears both happy and sad. I did not realize this until I experienced the loss of my dad. I also began to understand the post-partum depression that western medicine is now beginning to realize. Birth doulas and cultures where families stay with the mom and baby to assist in this transition heal much faster. These are traditions that can educate those willing to acknowledge the merit these have in post-partum care.

I have healed that partly with the unknowing help of my beautiful, kind daughter. I continue to heal the loss of two children from natural abortion. When I felt the quickening of the third pregnancy, I gave it the love I had not fully given before as I thought I was too old to care for another child. It only stayed for three weeks and then left. I felt so much guilt as well as grief. This has been a little more of a challenge for me. I've written letters to both, the second one I lost at eight weeks.

"When I am overwhelmed by everything that has
to get fixed in this broken-down world, show me
what is MINE to do then please give me the strength
to do it and the humility to rest afterwards."

—NADIA BOLZ-WEBER

I deeply appreciate quotes that remind me that if the world is "broken down," there is probably something in me that is as well. It is a challenge for me to let go of what is truly not mine to do. I am a caregiver, aren't I supposed to help everyone to heal? NO. It is about healing the spiritual, loving, kind, and compassionate Brenda. Then I can be quietly present to serve others simply. It is not about being on center stage and achieving accolades, nice as they may be. Those tend to get in the way of my connection to my heart's inner voice.

"I'm firmly convinced that true beauty springs from the acceptance of oneself, from an awareness of who we really are."

—PETER LINDBERGH

Many of us have a name for our divine connection like Goddess, God, Higher Power, Yahweh, Allah or... [add yours]. I grew up Catholic and always had a hard time with the name God. It felt hard to me with the hard sounding consonants. When I chose to participate in a 12-step life [I believe everyone would benefit], I kept asking what to call the divine as I have many I speak to. I was given Dear Ones because the initials are DO – listen and act. I laughed and thanked them. They do have a sense of humor. I consider myself a spiritual person, and currently I belong to no specific religion or church. I learn from all as each belief system has a new perspective on how to "be" the best I can today. There are so many ways to heal our grief, which is a blessing as we are all unique thus the process for each is unique.

I finished my master's degree in September 2000. My daughter was 24 living at home. We needed to cut the cord, and I needed a professional change. I was working at Kaiser Hospital as an Infection Control Coordinator for eighteen years. I requested a transfer to Kaiser Hawaii and was given a different job, one I was excited to learn. There was sorrow and guilt in this separation too. I knew Juli would be OK as she had our condo to live in and a job. She gave me a beautiful card dated 1/01 which says:

"Just as an experience stop, for a minute, and see yourself as I do. Step away from all that self-doubt, all the noise in your head, and notice how brave you are, how good, and how strong. Can you see it? Now LOOK deeper. There's more. A light about you, almost something that separates you from others. Your spirit shines. Stop for a minute. Believe. There is magic inside you."

—IMPROMPTU HALLMARK CARD

She wrote inside "Mom, I know this will be hard for both of us, but it will also do us both good. I know this is what you need to do right now, so I say go for it. I support you & will always be with... even if we are separated by an ocean! ♥ Juli." It brings tears twenty-five years later. I can feel her love and acceptance.

Reading this card with its beautiful message allowed me to show up at the new job, despite initial issues in my living situation and first day of orientation illness, with enthusiasm. It lifts me even today with reminders that my daughter and I are magical, compassionate, shining women uniquely sharing Love's Inner Voice with the world. Learning from grief and other challenges assist us along the way.

PONDER & JOURNAL

* What losses have I not recognized? What effect have they had on me?

* When does grief, guilt, or...show up in my life and how do I deal with it?

* What techniques assist me to acknowledge sadness or...and process it?

* Who is available for me to share my feelings with?

* Am I willing to learn, grow, possibly surrender or transform these low frequency feelings?

* What are my choices pertaining to...?

* What other questions or emotions have showed up?

DISCOVER **GRATITUDE**

I love the photo of me and my 98-year-old dad taken ten weeks before he passed peacefully on December 12, 2024. I am blessed and grateful to have had him in my life for three quarters of a century. He laughed and said "it is what it is" when I asked how he felt having a child that old.

I thought about sharing this under grief. Halfway through and with the assistance of SB Wade, I was challenged to travel through my grief with gratitude. I also wanted to start and end the writing of my "Discovery is Vital" journey with my dad.

"Instead of allowing grief to be the only emotion that defined the aftermath of my father's death, I embraced gratitude. This choice didn't negate the pain or the grief, but it introduced a new narrative. A story where every tear was a reminder of love, every memory a testament of a life well lived period."

—SB WADE "THE GRATITUDE EFFECT"

I highly recommend this book. It assisted me to evaluate how I wanted to continue living, be okay with crying, and taking a trip to Hawaii for deep healing without guilt.

My youngest brother, who lived close to my dad, and I shared the four-day vigil with a niece and dad's Hospice RN. The rest of the family, all at a distance, were there via phone calls and text. I appreciate that I had someone to share this journey with. We are the "bookends" of dad's seven children, me the eldest.

"Gratitude is not only the greatest of virtues, but the parent of all others."

—CICERO

GRATITUDE SYNONYMS – respect, appreciation, recognition, grace, praise

GRATITUDE ANTONYMS – thanklessness, ungratefulness, unappreciation

Looking over 2024 I realized that Dad had been slowly "fading" energetically for a while. It became noticeable from March 15, 2024, five years after mom's death. I respected my dad, his beliefs, and his willingness to share this time and conversations with me. We had some deep discussions about spirituality vs religion. He was a staunch Catholic throughout his life. I honored that and I think he honored my choice even if he didn't like it. I loved and appreciated these times together. I did go to church with him when I was visiting on a weekend. He appreciated my presence. We would usually enjoy a small meal at his home after if he was not too tired.

As his energy waned, he stayed home, going to a few activities but not out of the senior residence where he lived. He was loved and known by many who enjoyed his company and conversation, especially on philosophy and theology. My parents were avid bridge players, and he played bridge until two weeks before his death. He was grateful for all the activities offered and especially enjoyed the music gatherings. He had a wonderful voice. Most of our family sing or play an instrument. Mom gave us piano lessons. I sang in choirs and played cello in a youth symphony for which I am very grateful. Music heals me many times. Music energized dad. It was lovely to watch his enjoyment.

I like the thought of gratitude being a parent as Cicero said, like me and my dad. Gratitude is a high energy frequency and so easy to share. How easy is it to acknowledge someone in the store or on the street with a hello acknowledging their presence. Or even eye contact with a smile. I know it raises my energy when I do that. I enjoy noticing the responses if any, and it teaches me to let go of expectations about getting a response.

Due to dad's memory issues, I received weekly calls about mail and bills he received to be sure they were taken care of. I noticed that he started saying thank you after calls and visits in the last six months or so. It was lovely. I found it a gift that he appreciated my support and let go of the "duty" energy I used to feel. Like I had to show up as the eldest, the nurse, and a female. He learned that from his dad although he bucked his dad's teachings in many ways.

I saw gratitude in him for his life and for the coming transition at the same time. We talked about his "fading" with frankness. He was so grateful for the service he received and that he could easily attend communion every week, go to activities, have assistance to shower, and more.

Dad encouraged me to follow my dreams when I chose to live in Europe for nine months after working my first nursing job in Brooklyn New York. Mom was not happy. Dad was supportive in his unique way. I find this is also a time for looking back, like in a movie, watching with appreciation the encouragements and challenges given.

"Gratitude unlocks the fullness of life. It turns what we have into enough, and more. It turns denial into acceptance, chaos to order, confusion to clarity."

—MELODY BEATTIE

I sat vigil with many family members during mom's seven day passing journey in their apartment. I was with them when she passed while we were both sleeping. She knew dad would not be alone for the first time at night. She was able to go peacefully when I let her know I was with dad when she was ready to go. She left an hour later.

I experienced the grace and privilege of being present for both mom and dad in their transition. It was tearful and beautiful, another life paradox. Looking back, I recognized the depth these experiences brought to my life and heart, as they unlocked the "fullness of life" [Beatie] that mom and dad shared with me. Something only, I experienced. Each of my siblings had their own unique interaction with mom and dad.

I walk in gratitude for the life I have had so far thanks to my family. I am blessed.

I have come to realize that the ebb and flow of life are gifts to learn from, transform, accept, or let go. My journey continues to give me more self-awareness and appreciation for my divine inner voice of love. My prayer is that "Discovery is Vital-Awaken Love's Inner Voice" has assisted those who choose to awaken or deepen their own sacred connection.

PONDER & JOURNAL

* How difficult do I make it to find gratitude in challenges?

* How do I define gratitude?

* In what ways do I share/show my appreciation each day?

* Where can I shine gratitude, respect, kindness and compassion throughout my day?

DISCOVERY IS VITAL

SACRED ESSENCE
OF WORDS

H ere I am at the end of the many stories shared in this focused journal. Some of my stories have transformed, some I've surrendered,
and some have found homes within the confines of the focus words.

Notice how the words blend. I did have Divine assistance with the order in
which they are placed. I questioned a few, and as I kept writing, realized the
order is for the greatest good of all.

Rereading each chapter again and seeing the Dickinson quote in one of my
daily readers, I realized the connection is hope.

"'Hope' is the thing with feathers –
"That perches in the soul –
"And sings the tune without the words –

"And never stops – at all –"

—EMILY DICKINSON

I chose to start and finish my word stories with high frequency words to show myself and you dear readers, that Love's Inner Voice is about hope. For me each word has a gift to share when I am willing to listen and brings or enhances hope.

This is the first time hope has shown its light in this writing journey. For me, it is the perfect time and place. Each word story has hope built in, or something hopeful.

One of the primary synonyms for hope is purpose. Each word had a purpose toward growth, self-discovery, curiosity, and "being" in a new way, with Love's Inner Voice.

This has been a journey of light, love, and learning. Blessings to each of you, Brenda

PONDER & JOURNAL

Add your own now.

* What have I really learned?

* Is there anything I may still be hiding from?

* Are there any words I may need or wish to explore in a deeper way?

DISCOVERY IS VITAL

APPENDIX

EFT – Emotional Freedom Technic or tapping
https://eftinternational.org/

Dictionaries used throughout

      Marriam-Webster

      Oxford Language Dictionary

      Thesaurus.com

Havening - https://www.havening.org/

Medical News Review - https://www.medicalnewstoday.com/articles/core-beliefs

Quotes from various sources and each written as found.

Love's Inner Voice

Brenda L. Balding

ACKNOWLEDGMENTS

Ann Jonas – The Lotus Path and Love messenger – is an ongoing gift in my life. As a member of the Newreprenuership 101 success class she brings fun and light by sharing her own writing process and perspective as well as her

Sacred Connection nine-week experience. Thank you, Ann for sharing you with me and the world.

Lil Barcaski – GWN publishing, coach, and creator of Newreprenuership 101sucess class. I was privileged to be a member of the first iteration of her class. Lil assisted me with my article in the 2023 anthology *Sacred Connections* along with Ann Jonas, which Lil then published. Lil is very supportive, easy to work with, and is available to answer questions. My appreciation is beyond words Lil. Thank you.

Newreprenuership 101 class attendees for sharing their experiences during our class, especially related to the chapter questions Lil posed in our Guidebook to Success.

Deep appreciation for family members, and family of choice who support my *Discovery* journey of writing and publishing. Their support is unconditional acceptance.

Deep appreciation for sacred connection with my divine Dear Ones who assist me to walk my life journey one day at a time. They bless me.

I am grateful for each person in my life and those who choose to walk their own heart love self-discovery journey.

Blessings, Brenda

ABOUT THE AUTHOR

Brenda L Balding is a registered nurse of 50+ years and Reiki energy healer. She is also an author. spiritual guide, and self-discovery expert. Brenda is passionate about being in service to others and guides you on your path through some of life's challenges. Her focus via "Love's Inner Voice", is to support your self-discovery heart journey related to grief, should, acceptance, forgiveness, and others, as well as acknowledging emotions and feelings that show up along the way. Her mission is to encourage each person to enhance their own Love's Inner Voice, their sacred connection, for the greatest good of all.

Books: *Discovery is Recovery – Brain, Emotion and Spiritual Self-Reflection Through the Creative Process* and *Sacred Connection – Finding Our Path to Deeper Connection with Self and the Divine* an anthology that includes my article Sacred Discovery. Both are available on Amazon.com.